AFOOT
IN JAPAN

A Nineteenth Century Guide to
Walking The Back Roads

AFOOT IN JAPAN

A Nineteenth Century Guide to
Walking The Back Roads

❧

YASUMI ROAN

Translated by

WILLIAM SCOTT WILSON

For Ted Taylor

CONTENTS

I see a vision of a great rucksack revolution thousands or even millions of young Americans wandering around with rucksacks, going up to mountains to pray, making children laugh and old men glad, making young girls happy and old girls happier, all of 'em Zen Lunatics who go about writing poems that appear in their heads for no reason and also by being kind and also by strange unexpected acts keep giving visions of eternal freedom to everybody and to all living creatures . . .

—Jack Kerouac
The Dharma Bums, 1958

The word travel affects him like a waine-ox or a pack-horse. A carrier will carry him from any company that hath not been abroad. . . . A Dutch post doth ravish him. The mere superscription of a letter from Zurich sets him up like a top, Basle or Heildelberg make him spin. And at seeing the word Frankfurt or Venice, though but on the title of a book, he is ready to break doublet, crack elbows and overflow the room with his murmur.

—Ben Jonson on Thomas Coryat
c. 1616
Mathew Lyons
Impossible Journeys

Now is the time to visit all the celebrated places in the country and fill our heads with what we have seen, so that when we become old and bald we shall have something to talk about over the teacups.

—Ikku Jippensha
Hizakurige, 1802
Translated by Thomas Satchell

Whan that Aprill with his shoures sote The droughte of
Marche hath perced to the rote, And bathed every veyne
in swich licour, Of which vertu engendered is the flour;
Whan Zephirus eek with his swete breeth Inspired hath
in every holt and heath The tender croppes, and the yonge
sonne Hath in the Ram his half cours y-ronne; And small
fowles maken melodye That slepen al the night with open
ye—So priketh him Nature in her corages Than longen
folk to goon on pilgrimages.

—Geoffrey Chaucer
Canterbury Tales
c. 1400

In my loneliness,
      myself like floating duckweed,
roots loosened;
      were there inviting waters,
      I think I would go.

—Ono no komachi
c. 850

AFOOT
IN JAPAN

A Nineteenth Century Guide to
Walking The Back Roads

PREFACE

BY WILLIAM SCOTT WILSON

Some years ago, I was hiking over one of the steeper passes on the Kisokaido, an ancient road running between modern Tokyo and Kyoto. It was an early autumn morning, the air was clear and crisp, and chestnuts lay all about the path, some already opened and eaten by the wild pigs and black bears that still thrive in the mountains of Central Japan. I was in my 50s at the time, felt that I was making good progress as I climbed towards the top of the pass, but was looking forward to a rest at the old Shinto shrine that had been established there centuries before.

As I worked my way up the path, however, I could faintly hear something or somebody gradually coming up behind me treading over the dry leaves and chestnut husks. I was equipped with one of the little brass bells provided in the villages along the way which were said to scare away any wild animals, but still felt a slight edge of anxiety. Looking over my shoulder, I saw, instead of a bear or wild pig, a man of medium build who appeared to be in his mid or late 70s, quickly gaining ground on me with a light but energetic step. Stopping to talk, we exchanged pleasantries about the fine weather and the beauty of the area. His name was Matsumoto, he said, and he was just out for a morning hike. He was equipped with a walking stick, a bell and a light pack, and so couldn't be going far, I thought. When I asked him his destination, however, it turned out to be three villages beyond where I would stop, or a distance of about twenty miles. I might add that he was not breathing nearly as heavily as I was, though to be fair, my pack weighed close to fifty pounds, filled with the stuff I would need for three weeks on the road. We soon parted to take advantage of the day, and as I carried on, saw him quickly disappear up ahead of me over a slight rise and around a corner. When I arrived at the shrine and took off my pack some fifteen minutes later, he was long gone. Likely, he was already well on his way down the pass, headed for the next village, where he would enjoy a quick mid-morning bowl of noodles and be on his way.

Mr.Matsumoto was not the first or last hiker I met on the back roads of Japan, but was in fact, one of the many modern inheritors of what has been called the "road culture" of the Edo period.

· ∽ ·

Some two hundred and fifty years before Jack Kerouac had had his vision of "thousand or even millions of young Americans wandering around with rucksacks," there was a historic cultural shift in Japan that witnessed people of every social stripe on the road, sometimes for weeks or even months, out for the sheer pleasure of being out and away from their everyday lives. With the Battle of Sekigahara in 1600, more than one hundred and fifty years of disruptive civil wars came to an end, brigandage nearly disappeared, official government roads maintained by the local war lords were established, local barriers were demolished, and the economy boomed. Although passports and travel passes were required for travel through the few central government barriers, the distribution and regulation of such documents were often loosely regulated, and at times, so many pilgrims stood in line at the barrier gates that the guards threw up their hands and let them all through. In the hierarchy of scrutiny at these barriers, the war lords and their families received the most attention, while prostitutes and entertainers barely required even the semblance of official papers.

As the number of travelers increased on the roads, so did the number of inns, tea houses, noodle restaurants and souvenir shops to accommodate them. Which, in turn, made it possible for even more people to be traveling. Thus, war lords and their entourages, masterless samurai, merchants, wandering priests and poets, entertainers, farmers, groups of women and even shop boys who left without permission, walked, rode on horseback or were carried in palanquins along the great roads by the thousands. In time, this led to a great cross-section of ideas and local cultures, and came to help redefine what it meant to be Japanese. This was reflected especially in literature, and by the early 1800s, detailed guide books were published making travel all the more convenient.

For people who had spent their entire lives in their villages, towns or the great cities like Edo, Kyoto and Osaka, however, correct preparations for such outings were not fully understood; and unfortunate events connected with proper attire, local food, proper etiquette, local customs and wild animals eventually led to the publication of books and pamphlets like Yasumi Roan's *Ryoko yojinshu*,

Written and published in 1810, this short book includes tips and information on a myriad subjects: from footwear, changes in water, prevention of seasickness, poisonous bugs, what to wear in colder climates, what to do if you fall off a horse, to how to prevent fatigue.

And while some of the topics may seem dated or inappropriate for modern hikers, I would urge the reader to think broadly, and try to imagine how what appears to be antiquated advice may apply to modern times. Travelling on foot in an unfamiliar environment presents many of the same problems to the Japanese as it does to the Westerner who decides to get off the beaten path in Japan today. Thus the periodic republication of this two hundred year old book in both the original and modern Japanese—my two copies were printed in 1972 and 2009—and this translation as well.

Never, it is said, dismiss anything out of hand.

* * *

I have omitted a few sections of the book that I thought would be either tedious or, in fact, truly outdated. One such section lists a number of Chinese medicines and their ingredients that are very unlikely to be found even in the most traditional medicines shops today. The ingredients, too, were so arcane that only a few were to be found even in my 13-volume dictionary, Morohashi's *Dai kanwa jiten*. Also not translated is the long list of hot springs, the majority of which have long ceased to exist, and a chart of the hours of sunrise and sunset throughout the month. All of the other information, however, should be either useful, culturally informative, or in some way interesting to the modern reader and/or traveler, whether the latter be journeying through either urban or rural Japan.

INTRODUCTION

BY YASUMI ROAN

When people have some time off from their work and think about setting off on a pilgrimage to the Ise shrine, they will invite friends to accompany them, determine an auspicious day for departure, receive parting gifts from here and there, and make preparations cheerfully throughout the house. All of this somehow braces up the traveler's mood. Finally, when the day arrives, family and friends come to see him off at the edge of town, sake is passed around, relatives offer various kinds of advice about being on the road, and seen from the side it is all quite enviable.

Again, nothing braces up the mind or tightens the body like departing for trips here and there for work or some business, regardless of the traveler's age.

People from the eastern part of Japan think about visiting Ise first of all, then Yamato, Kyoto, Osaka, Shikoku, and Kyushu, and viewing the famous places, historical sites, Shinto Shrines and Buddhist temples in all of these places. People from the western part of the country would like to make the rounds from Ise to Edo, Kashima, Katori, Nikko, Matsushima in Oshu, Kisagata, and the Zenkoji Temple in Shinshu.

When everyone in the household is healthy and work is going well, the master of the house, naturally enough, but also the retainers and relatives, will make the pilgrimage to Ise Shrine at least once in their lives. In Japan, this is a happy custom handed down from generation to generation.

Regardless of social rank, whether a person be a samurai, farmer, craftsman or merchant, if he works diligently and honestly day in and day out, he will accredit his peaceful life and pleasant circumstances and lack of hunger to the teachings of the gods and buddhas.

Regardless of whether one is born into a wealthy or aristocratic home, if he is naturally weak, he will be unable to walk the mountains and hills while viewing rare scenery or climb to the sacred places on the peaks. Of course, if you would speak of money, it is true that a person may travel riding in a palanquin. But the joy of travel for a [wealthy] sickly person, will not come close to that of a poor but healthy man, and this is surely regrettable.

At any rate, regardless of whether one has money or not, there is no greater happiness than making a pilgrimage in good health.

By the way, for the person who leaves on a journey, there is something he should understand from the day of his departure, and this is in taking care of his own daily outfit, such as his drawers and straw sandals. Also, even if one is not filled or satisfied with his morning or evening meals, he should eat with restraint. No matter what the affair, he must think individually that it is an opportunity for pursuing knowledge.

Also, depending on the area in which the traveler stays, the customs may be different, and he may not be received in a manner fitting his mood. He should understand this well beforehand, or he may make serious mistakes.

Various difficulties may arise while on the road: one may meet with wind and rain, the circumstances may be that a deep mist envelopes the mountain one crosses from the early morning, the night clothing provided may be thin, there may be fights between fellow travelers, someone's feet may hurt so that they cannot make good progress along the road, or the weather may change and people get sick. In such cases, it will be difficult to redress the situation as quickly as one might at home.

Thus, it is difficult to express the hardships of an extended trip.

For this reason, it is said that travel is educational for the young; as the old saying goes, "Have your cherished child go on a journey." Certainly it is true that, regardless of being rich or poor, the person who had never travelled will be unaware of this kind of hardship, and will think that travel is just for pleasure and happy excursions through the mountains. Such people may be unacquainted with human-heartedness and selfishness, and laughingly be pointed at behind their backs.

Even warlords and aristocrats of high rank, regardless of encountering strong rains, will head out to their determined lodging for the night as long as they are not stopped by flooding rivers. All the more so, the common traveler should just pass along on his own whim.

In this way, anyone who adjusts to adversity with human-heartedness and maintains a mind of sympathy will be noted by society as a good person, will succeed in life, and guarantee prosperity for his descendants. Surely this gives credence to the teaching, "Have your cherished child go on a journey."

I have loved traveling since I was young, have taken journeys here and there, and my friends and acquaintances who knew about these trips have asked me for bits of information every time I've gone out. For this reason, I have written various things down here and pass them on. Now recently I've gotten old, but still feel that I shouldn't refuse writing something about each trip. Thus, I have gathered together all of my notes into one volume along with what I remember of the information I took down on various trips. Hoping that this will be of at least a little use to others, I have printed this with the title, *Afoot in Japan*.

Yasumi Roan
June, 1810

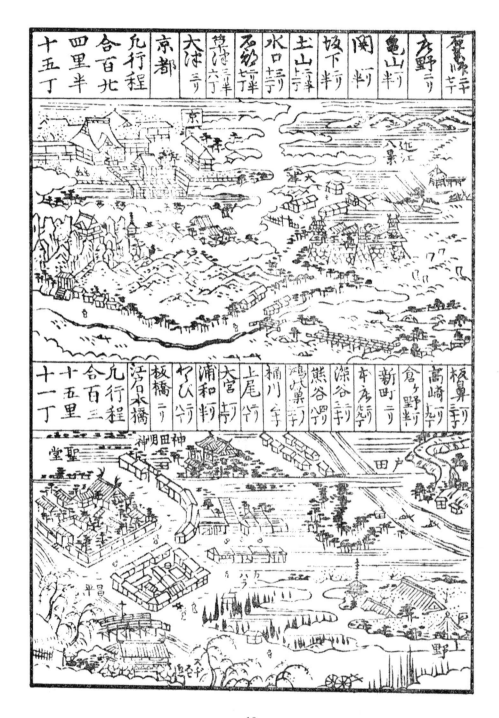

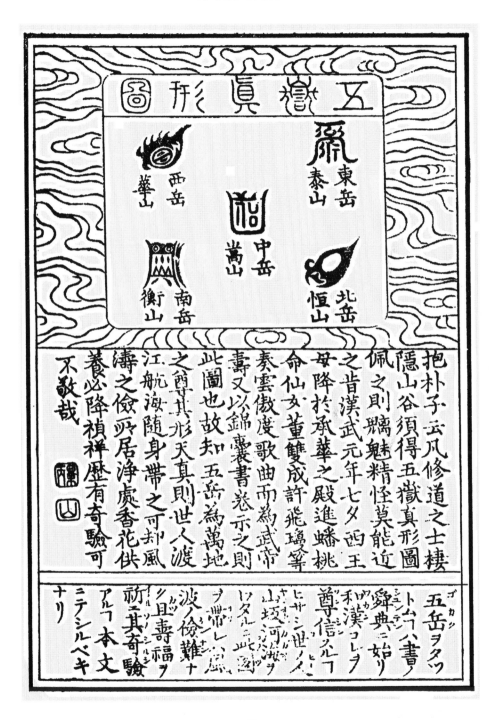

Sixty-one Tips on Travel

On the first day of a journey, step out firmly but calmly, making sure that your footwear has adapted itself to your feet. For two or three days after starting out, rest from time to time, so that your feet won't hurt. At first, anyone will be impatient and walk along recklessly without a thought of taking a break. But if your feet start to hurt, you will suffer a good bit during your trip. At any rate, it is essential that you are attentive to your feet from the very beginning

Other than what you can put in a small pack, the things that you carry along on a journey should be very few You may think that you need to bring a lot of things, but in fact, they will only become troublesome.

When you arrive at your lodging, it is necessary to first ask about and confirm the directions of north, south, east and west; and then check out the building's construction, the location of the toilet, and the exits and entrances both front and back. This has been taught since ancient times. This is done in the case of a nearby fire, a thief breaking and entering, or a fight breaking out.

When a person is traveling for the first time, and he needs horses, palanquins or coolies, he should make these requests from the master of the inn the night before. If you negotiate with the pack horse driver or palanquin carriers directly, things are likely to go badly on the road. The person who is carrying the receipt ledger should hand it over to the proper person at the inn, and rely on him. Announce to the inn people the night before what the departure time will be on the following day, and give yourself the margin to be on time. If the inn people have not awakened on time, wake them up and make yourself ready to go—even in tying on your straw sandals—by the time breakfast is prepared. Only then, eat your morning meal. If you do not do this, the preparations for the horses and coolies will also be neglected, you will be delayed, and things will not go well. Regardless of social standing, when you travel, if you do not take care of this, preparations will be poorly done.

In the morning, everyone is bustling about, and there is the likelihood of forgetting something. For this reason, look over your belongings at night, think about what you need and don't need, and put things in order. If you have to do things like look for your socks under your bedding, your morning departure will be delayed. And if your morning departure is slowed down, the rest of the day will be also.

As for lodging, as is the rule for determining designated inns, but also for inns in areas you are traveling for the first time and do not know well, lodge in inns that are well constructed and prosperous. It is best to do this even if the places are a little more expensive.

When traveling, you should try to protect yourself from the heat and cold. Be especially careful during the summer. When it's hot, the condition of the stomach and intestines worsens, and it is more difficult to digest your food. Thus, you should not eat a lot of unfamiliar fish, fowl, shellfish, bamboo shoots, mushrooms, melons, watermelons, mocha or red rice. During the summer you can be discomforted with everything from upset stomach to sunstroke. You should consider the summer as a study point for the spring, autumn and winter.

Do not overeat in the middle of a journey just because you're hungry. It is especially inadvisable to eat in a hurry. First calm down, then eat. If you're horribly hungry, you'll suffer from cardiac fatigue, and over-eating at such a time will make you feel ill or make you sick all of a sudden. You should consider this well.

Do not drink sake on an empty stomach, but go ahead and drink after your meal. It is better to heat your sake and then drink it in either hot or cold weather.

You should not recklessly drink shochu on a journey. This is because there are times when you can actually get food poisoning. If it's high class shochu, you can drink a little. That said, during the long rains of the summer or in damp areas, drinking a little shochu or rice brandy may pick up your spirits a little. Nevertheless, you should not imbibe such drinks in the fall or winter.

You should not get into the bath when your stomach is empty. Wait for a little while after your meal, then get in. However, if there are a lot of people [at the inn], and you'll interfere with others taking their baths after you, just be careful, first wet your feet, and then submerge yourself, even if your stomach is empty.

If you go to take a bath in an inn where there are other guests, be sure to follow the instructions of the innkeeper. In a busy inn, it is possible to mix up the proper order in using the bath, and that can easily cause an argument. At such a time, look carefully at the other guests; if someone appears to be a person of high status, let him take his bath before you. At any rate, being mistaken about the order of using the bath can result in fights. In all cases, if you will be reserved in all matters when on a journey, you will often be better off.

清輔

ゆくま、に
花の梢と
なりにけり
よそに
見へつる
峯の
しら雪

16

When you are extraordinarily tired, soaking in a hot bath for longer than is usual for you will relieve your fatigue. However, do not wash your face a number of times when you are sitting in the tub. This will cause a rush of blood to your head (and make you feel dizzy).

On an ordinary trip, if you are not in a particular hurry, you should never walk at night. No matter what kind of trip you are on, there will be a number of good points to planning to walk a nine-day journey in ten, including not walking hurriedly at night. Also, when crossing a river, you should not think only of your own convenience.

Be very circumspect about sexual desire when traveling. Prostitutes carry sexually transmitted diseases, and these are frighteningly easily transmitted during hot weather. Also, because skin diseases can be contracted from bedding, be sure to wear some fragrance on your body.

On journeys during the summer, you sometimes get thirsty and drink water, but you should drink water only if it's clean. Even if it is from old ponds or flowing forth from a mountain, if it is not clear running water it should not be drunk indiscriminately. This can definitely do you harm. You should drink water while taking *Goreizan.** You should also carry Japanese and regular pepper. Such medicines will counter bad mountain air and humidity.

When traveling during the summer, there are people who, when becoming exhausted, will lie down and rest or sleep in the grass by the side of the road, but you should by no means do this. The summer fields are full of poisonous insects. and even if the insect itself is not poisonous, it may come in contact with something that is, and when stung by such an insect, that poison can be quite strong. Moreover, you should not rest for a long time in the thick forests around old shrines and temples, in caves, by riversides or damp

---

* A traditional Chinese medicine composed of five ingredients. Used as a cure for fever, dry throat, and urinary problems. Even today it is used for edema, nephritis, hangover and autointoxication.

places just because they seem cool. Much harm can result from the humidity in such places.

You should absolutely not walk hurriedly after a meal. If you're riding a horse or traveling in a palanquin, you should not go too fast. If your palanquin turns over or you fall from your horse, the food you have eaten will not settle in your stomach, and you would have to be careful not to get dizzy and faint.

When you need to answer the call of nature, you should practice self-control, and never relieve yourself if you are on horseback or riding in a palanquin. Falling from a horse could tax your heart, and might result in death.

If you're going to have the lodging at a destination ahead make arrangements for coolies or horses, send word for them to go two or three days before your [planned] departure. If you do not, you may encounter them on the way, and they will thus be of no use.

There are many poisonous plants that grow in the summer fields, and you may encounter poisonous insects as well, so you should note this down. Everyone knows that the *mamushi* (a kind of pit viper, *Agkistrodonblomhoffi*) and the tiger beetle (either the *Cincindela japonica* or the *Epicauta gorhami*) are quite poisonous. There are other insects, however, that are poisonous only during certain seasons, and their poison is in no way inferior to that of snakes and scorpions. Therefore, one should be careful about certain kinds of gnats, mosquitoes, horseflies, wasps, ants, caterpillars, spiders and leeches. In hot areas, the humidity and temperatures can be especially horrific, and harbor many poisonous plants and strange insects. Thus, travelers should be very careful about resting in the fields when tired. (Illustrations, pgs. 19 & 20)

When a warrior's baggage—or even the baggage of a merchant—arrives at a post town, first greet the official in charge politely, take out the register and declare the number of men and horses involved. Next, make sure that the baggage that has been delivered is in order, and speak quietly with the man in charge. The post town's shipping agency may be in a disorderly condition, so be careful not to lose anything or be rude to anyone.

類ひに至る迄用心すへ
きことなり。温熱の地
は暑湿別而甚しく、毒
草、異虫も多き故、旅
人つかれて山野に休む
とも、是等の心得ある
へきことなり。毒虫に
さ、れたる妙薬等ハ、
末のくすりの所にあり。

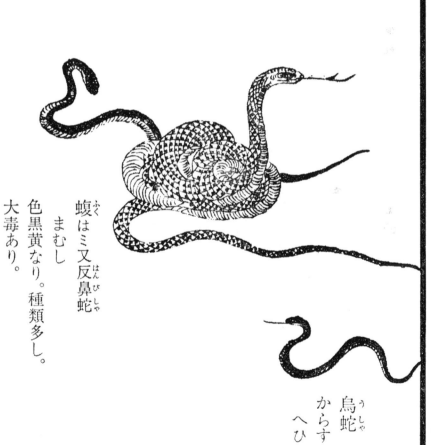

蝮はミ又反鼻蛇
まむし
色黒黄なり。種類多し。
大毒あり。

烏蛇
からす
へひ

夏の原野に生る毒草、
毒虫、数多けれバ挙て
尽すべからず。就中蝮、
斑猫の大毒なること八、
皆人の知ところ也。其
外諸虫の中、無毒虫に
ても折に触て毒あるも
のにあふ時ハ、蛇蝎に
もをとらぬものあり。
よって蚹、蚊、虻、蜂、
蟻、蚚蜤、蜘蛛、蛭の

唐斑猫
色微黄
和斑猫
色るり也。

蜥蜴和名 とかけ
石竜子
山竜子　同物

For a warrior or even a merchant, if he is journeying on an important business for his master, it is important to be patient even if things do not go satisfactorily with the horse packers or coolies. If this endangers his duties, that is one thing; but if not, you should understand that patience is the first policy. Again, understand that being delayed on the road undermines the meaning of a journey for your master.

During a journey, there are times when baggage must be unloaded for a change of coolies and horses. For the traveler, however, this is an annoying delay, and is felt to be a great nuisance. One must be resolved, and when the horse packers are in a hurry and replacing the baggage, the traveler himself must be ready to help with this in order to be sure that small packages will not fall off the pack horses and that the number of strings of money is correct.

When you pack clothing and folded paper in wicker baskets, wrap them in two layers of oiled paper, packing them so that what is inside will not get wet. Crossing a river, water will enter in the space between the basket and the lid. And you should take this kind of care, not just with wicker baskets but also with wicker containers held on shoulder poles. Generally speaking, you should be careful not to dampen and lose things at river crossings. You can safely use wicker materials made at the Suruga-ya, located in front of Dentsu-In in Edo.

When you encounter an unfamiliar river on your journey, you should never cross it on foot. Still, when a bridge has been washed away by a flood, there are times when you must cross the river either on foot or on a boat. On such occasions, you should discuss the matter with a post town official. You should not negotiate this on your own. Discuss matters in all situations, and everything should go well.

If you are travelling with women and you must cross a river, you should make preparation [beforehand]. Because women are different than men and tend to be nervous, they will look at the river and will be afraid of the power and energy of the water, be shocked at the rough attitude of the coolies who carry them across, and from time to time become faint-hearted. Thus, if you plan to cross a river, it is best to explain in full the day before how crowded [the boat] may be, and explain that she should not become alarmed even if she is separated from [the man] who accompanies her. In such situations there will no worries if someone like the post town official is present, but women are timid and when faced with difficult locations like river crossings, and even being at the water's edge, boat crossings and mountain paths, it is essential to explain things beforehand.

At river crossings* and boat crossings, be careful with the things in your purse or pockets. Also, there are times when things placed in the palanquin will fall out, and if something falls into the water, it will be difficult to find.

There are times when a horse is also boarded on a boat that people share. At such times, the horse should be boarded first, and the people afterward. If people board first, the horse will not want to get on the boat, become unruly, and perhaps injure someone. Also, it is far better if the elderly and women do not go onto a boat that is carrying a horse.

You should be careful about using a boat just because you think it will be the route of less distance. When you have to hurray because of some important business, you should go by land as much as possible. If you're not in a hurry, it's good to board a boat and rest your feet, and if you have an unexpected following wind, all will go well. But if something unusual should occur, you'll know the meaning of the old saying, "Regret never comes first."

For a flooding river, no matter how small, it will not do to make light of it and cross it without care. The force of a flooding river is not only exceptionally strong, but there are various things being swept along in the current that can cause grave injuries. Also, rivers that are close by mountains—even if they appear to be ordinarily small rivers with little water—when snow melts or there is a sudden storm deep in the mountains, there will be a sudden increase in the amount of water, the width of the river can suddenly increase and a permanent bridge cannot be built. Plank bridges are built for use only in winter,

---

* "River crossing" will generally mean being carried across a river on the back of a coolie, or in a palanquin.

22

but are washed away during floods. Rivers like the Sakawagawa on the Tokaido, the Shirazawa on the Ooshukaido, and rivers in Odawara are like this. There are many rivers like this particularly in mountainous provinces. It goes without saying that during flooding of this sort, you should not attempt to wade across the river on foot, but neither should you try to make a crossing on a plank bridge that can be seen out in the middle of the river. There are cases where people have been swept away crossing a floating bridge set by stakes during floods.

It happens often that, after a long continuing rain, a mountain will collapse and cause landslides. In times like this, never stay in an inn situated beneath a large crag or on a riverbank. Set your mind to this beforehand, and think in terms of your journey.

When you have travelling companions, and there are wages to pay the coolies or horse packers, or the bill for lodging, do so each time with each paying his own. If some do not have the small currency [necessary], and you pay [for them] just that time, be sure to make the settlement wherever you stop at the end of the day. On a long journey, the money that is borrowed and lent, even if it is recorded in a journal, will end in confusion. One should not be foolish on this account.

If you fall in with travelling companions for three, or even five or six days, you should not stay in the same lodging, eat together or share the same medicine, even if they seem like trustworthy people.

When you are inconvenienced because you do not have a horse, and you encounter someone with a packhorse already loaded up, even if he should be someone you know, it is better not to request that your own baggage be added on. Should you suddenly need some of your baggage on the way, it will be on this other man's horse and there will not be time. Any traveler should be resolved to take strict responsibility for his own belongings while on the journey, and not rely on others to carry them for him.

If you travel with companions, they should at the most number only five or six people. It is not good to go with a large crowd. People have different inclinations, and on a long trip in a large crowd, inharmonious situations are going to arise.

People you should not travel with include heavy drinkers, those with unsavory habits, hot-tempered people, asthmatics, or the chronically ill. You never know when these infirmities are going to occur, so it's better to think this over well.

If you are on foot and carrying the expenses for your journey, you should keep them in a money belt inside your clothing at your waist. Money for the day's expenses can be carried in a wallet and brought out in small amounts. Of course, it is essential that even at night, those small amounts should be dispensed out of the sight of others.

When you stay overnight at an inn, both your sword and dagger should be placed beneath the bed in which you sleep. Weapons like spears and halberds should also be put at the back of your bed.

On a journey you should be especially mindful of fire. Naturally enough, when you pass through a village, but also when going through fields or plains, you should not wantonly toss away your tobacco ashes. When you are resting or riding on a boat, clothing and baggage will catch on fire. You should be very careful about this.

During the spring, farmers will purposefully burn their fields* here and there. These fires will spread at surprising speed in a strong wind. When you pass through places like this, consider well which road you should take. Even a main road can be surrounded by fire. Do not make light of this.

You should not idly reach out your hands for fruits like Japanese pears, persimmons, citrons and mandarin oranges being grown at houses or gardens by the side of the road, no matter how ripe and plentiful they are.** And of course, you should not mistakenly step on grains inside a village or garden that are being laid out to dry. If people complain about your actions in an area not your own, you will not come out on the best side of the argument, be you right or wrong..

---

* This is done in early spring both to kill off insects and create ashes for fertilizer.

** Don't tie your shoes in a melon patch; don't adjust your hat under a pear tree. (Zen saying)

都にはまた
青葉
にて
見しか
もみぢ散　とも
しく
しら川の
せき
頼政

When you encounter young ladies, female grass cutters, or women in a group that is crossing your path in the mountains or on a path across the fields, it is best to offer a simple greeting but not to follow up with any more useless talk. Also, you should not thoughtlessly laugh at the countrified expressions of someone you may meet [on the road]. Be aware that trouble may begin from trivialities.

You will not feel good if you have to stay overnight in an unpleasant inn in a mid-post town village or in a place off the main road. Nevertheless, make no complaints at such a time, speak more calmly than you would ordinarily, very carefully put away your own baggage, and fasten the doors to your room. This is a secret to travelling.

When anyone goes to an area unfamiliar to him, [he will find that] various ways of speaking and customs will be different. As the words are different from the place where he lives, he will be unaccustomed to hearing them, and unaccustomed to seeing what is around him. Though he will think these things to be strange, it is certain that the people of [this unfamiliar area] will think the same of him. It is a mistake to be unaware of this and to laugh at the customs and language of another place. To laugh at and distain another's words or phrasing can be the source of an altercation.

If a person is walking along the road singing Noh drama chants, ballads or puppet play songs to himself, you should not sing along with him. This is also the source of altercations.

Things that you should not stop to look at while on the road: fights, arguments, gambling, games of *go* or *shogi*, village dances, village sumo matches, a person accidentally killed, or the place where someone was killed. By and large, you should not stop and gaze at places where many people have gathered together.

In cases where you have some other business than commerce or are taking a hot springs cure, when you are on a pilgrimage, or times when you must stay at an inn because there has been a suspension of ferry service, do not get involved in any risky or speculative business, and for sure do not join any games of *go* or *shogi* for stakes. Moreover, do not become involved even in some business that you know.

Problems arise from desire for profit, disasters come to life, and these cause great delays. You must be cautious of such things.

There is much sulfur in the atmosphere at hot springs, and the blades and fittings of both long and short swords will rust. You must be careful about this. There are places where this will not happen, but in many, rust is a problem . . .

When on a journey concerning business for your master or in starting some great enterprise, do not take some roundabout way—regardless of how short—in order to visit a famous historical site. Moreover, never take unfamiliar shortcuts or take a shorter route by boat.

If you are in your inn and a fire breaks out nearby, quickly collect your clothes, take everything that is important around you, check the direction of the wind, then grab your baggage and go. Have whatever attendants there are light lamps, give instructions to those carrying things and running out, and make sure that nothing has been lost or left behind. At such times, do not depend on the guidance of the people working at the inn.

It's well and good to share an inn with other people when on a journey, and if you yourself will be fully careful, all will go well. Most importantly, be sure to fasten your door, and quickly ascertain the appearance of the other guests. If there is a vicious drinker or someone with a strange way about him, be prepared for what may happen. There are not a few examples of unpleasant events occurring in inns shared with other people.

If a drinking party has begun in an inn you are sharing with other people and it goes on until late at night, have the companions you are with stay awake and keep watch one by one until the drinking party has ended. Difficult situations also arise from drawn-out drinking parties.

Horses are easily frightened, and if frightened, may jerk or buck. At such a time, do not become flustered and leap off of the horse. Look carefully and determine if the baggage is about to slide off, then dismount. If you lose your presence of mind and leap off the horse, you will likely injure yourself.

28

If you are riding on a horse from the countryside during March or April, be especially careful when dismounting. Such horses are not used every day, are kept at rest, and ridden only occasionally. Allured by the bright liveliness of spring, they are liable to frolic and dash about. Ride them with care.

Be careful when riding horses during the summer, as they may be stung by horseflies and sometimes buck. Again, people riding on horses in the summer may become sleepy, and this is dangerous. For this reason, you should be careful on mountainous slopes and riverbanks. The elderly and children should be particularly careful.

If a guest at the inn where you are lodging offers to sell you some miracle drug at a cheap price, firmly refuse and make no purchase. If you need medicine, have it prepared at a pharmacy.

A courier or supervisor in charge of sending baggage must understand the importance of his position, regardless of how heavy or light the items are. Letters and documents are more important than gold and silver, and if they should somehow fall and be lost, not only will the sender be at a loss, but something important may fall into another's hands. One must be careful about this.

The swords you wear at your side on a journey should be light and short. You should not carry a long *katana* or *wakizashi** or a gaudy sheath, wear unusual clothing, or display outstanding possessions. An outstanding appearance invites disaster.

Retainers, man servants and other employees that accompany you on a trip should call their families together before the departure, and each write a document stating that the proper measures will be taken on the event of that person should fall sick and die on the journey. Should the worst happen, and someone should die of an illness on the way, the doctor and innkeeper should also write documents concerning the event. As a supplement, if you are on a journey by yourself, traveling through different provinces, you should carry a document

---

* *Katana*: The standard long sword. *Wakizashi*: The short sword. Samurai wore both at their waist.

stating that you are a parishioner of such and such a Buddhist temple. In this way, the person who has thought through everything will be someone for whom disasters will not arise.

If you are on the road and a solar eclipse occurs, rest for a while, then continue walking after the eclipse has done its course. The same goes for a lunar eclipse.

It goes without saying that it is absolutely forbidden to scribble, write or post bills on shrines and temples, but also on bridges, standing trees and huge rocks.

Particularly important matters other than the sixty-one articles noted above are written in detail below.

Concerning Caution on the

Change of Water

nyone who travels to a foreign province will find that his stomach does not feel well after a few days due to the change in water. And, along with the specific problems of hot flushes, constipation, or rashes, he may also suffer from other ailments.

Of course a foreign province will be composed of the same land and sky, and as one breathes the same air, it would seem that a change in water would not be such a concern; but this is not so. Depending on the natural features of every area, not only water, but heat and cold, climate, the character of the people and even the food all have more differing aspects than one could count.

雪ふれはミな高からぬ
山もなしいつれかこしの
しらねなるらむ　師時

For example, when river fish are put in a pond on level ground, after a while they seem to be puzzled or at a loss. Now, when people are put in the climate of a foreign area and are not acclimated to it for one or two months, they will surely become ill. One should be careful about this.

The climate of the Kanto area* is fundamentally different from that of Kyoto and Osaka. Moreover, if you go as far as the western provinces and Kyushu, the climate changes there as well. Again, the northern provinces, Echigo and the area of the deep north are extraordinarily different. And if you go to the coastline or the islands, the place names and topography are different yet again, so you can imagine how different [their climates] are.

Thus, when a person from a warm area goes to a cold one, he is stricken by the cold weather. It is rare, however, that a person going to a warm area from a cold one will be affected.

Many years ago, when a large number of people from the island of Hachijo moved to Edo, they were met with an outbreak of smallpox and measles, and many of them died. This was certainly because they had not adapted to the land [and climate].

Because of such things, people who are stationed in a faraway land, or those going on trips to hot springs, should be careful about their food and drink and their daily activities for about two weeks from the day of their departure. I will write in detail about the medicines you may take while on the road at the end of the book.

---

* The Kanto: the area around Tokyo, or Edo as it was called in Roan's time.

Understanding Travel in Cold Provinces

When traveling in the deep northern provinces* you should be very careful from the time you eat your morning meal. In cold districts, snow falls daily from the beginning of the Ninth Month and accumulates more and more every day around the time of the Festival of Ebisu,** burying the mountains and fields. Moreover, the snow in these cold places is for the most part quite powdery, and even on days when it doesn't snow, the wind blows so that conditions are much like a blizzard. And of course, on days that it does snow, it piles up to one or two feet right before your eyes. Furthermore, the tracks of other people on the road completely disappear from sight.

---

*　奥羽 and北越.

** The Festival of Ebisu: When merchants prayed for prosperity, calling in specialists to celebrate Ebisu, one of the Seven Happy Gods. Commonly celebrated on November 20th, but in some places on October 20th.

34

For someone who is stepping out on official business, he should employ coolies and have them show him the way. There is no reason why the general traveler should do this, however, and you rarely run into people from whom you can get directions. There are many people who lose their way, are unable to find the correct road, and end up completely lost.

Accordingly, even a person who is able to drink sake should never drink a lot. Drinking much sake makes the body feel warm, and the person will think that something like a blizzard is a small matter. The fields and mountains will be covered with snow; the rice paddies, vegetable gardens and, naturally enough, the roads will disappear, and as far as one can see will appear to be level land. There are many cases when, under the influence of alcohol, a man will wander around without a sense of direction, fall into a deep gutter or ditch, and freeze to death. The roads are especially unclear at night.

Therefore, you should eat well at breakfast time. In addition, you should carry some fried rice for a noon meal, and be careful not to go out on an empty stomach. With no food in your stomach, you will be done in by the cold, your energy and strength will be exhausted, and in the end you will collapse during a blizzard.

If you do not drink sake, you will not lose your life even if you are wrapped in a blizzard until dawn. The fact that there have been many occasions when people have frozen to death in blizzards in the deep northern districts is due to drinking sake, and a lot of it.

To warm up people who have been caught in a blizzard and nearly frozen, becoming numb in their hands and feet or feeling unwell, you should light a fire with straw, and put it at a distance from them at first.

Moreover, when you put someone who has been completely frozen in a bath, the water should be just lukewarm at first, then heated up only gradually. When suddenly warmed by a hot fire or hot water, a person may feel dizzy and lose consciousness.

Equipment for Traveling in Cold Districts

W hen traveling in snow, undergarments made of paper,* quilted cotton, or leather are good. There are not enough words to describe the terrible cold and the depth of the snow in snow country.

The boots and straw sandals used in snow country will not be available in your own province, so even if you prepare for such things ahead of time, they will not be of use in the place where you are going.

---

* Paper garments: clothes made of prepared *washi*, or Japanese paper. Sometimes lacquered with persimmon, and used as rain gear.

Natetsuki in Cold Provinces

W hen you travel in the deep north, there are places here and there where mountains tower above both sides of the road for distances of two or three or even four or five ri.*

In the spring of a year of heavy snows, around the equinox in the Second Month, the snow on the mountains on both sides of the road will begin to melt from the season's warmth. Then, with either an east wind, thunder, an earthquake or the reverberations of tree branches rustling together, the accumulated snow on both towering mountainsides will crash down on the mountain roads all at once. In the provincial dialect, this is called a *natetsuki*, or avalanche.

---

* One *ri* is approximately equivalent to approximately 2.44 miles.

From time to time, people traveling on mountain roads are crushed beneath such avalanches, and often meet with sudden deaths. There is no way to protect yourself from a disaster like this.

Moreover, even when others receive word that a number of people have met with and been crushed beneath an avalanche, they are unable to quickly dig through the snow and recover the bodies. Other than waiting for the snow to melt in the summer, there is nothing to be done.

People on business for their masters or on important errands should never travel in places like this. They should pass through only upon researching the temperatures on the days before and after the journey through, and making inquiries of the locals. Natives of these areas will tell you that, when you *do* go, you should tread lightly, be careful about coughing, and to walk with prudence.

There are stone monuments from the disasters of these avalanches all along the mountain roads between Aizu and Echigo, and between Joshu and Mikuni.

How to Avoid Various Wild Animals

in the Mountains

W hen people are travelling with companions in the deep mountians and fields, the bears and wolves hear their voices and hide. But a single traveler will not be talking, and if a wild animal is sleeping by the roadside and unexpectedly encounters a human being, it will be alarmed and sometimes bite him. In broad daylight such things do not happen, but often happen at night.

Thus, when walking through the mountains or fields and plains far from human habitation, make noises as you walk, striking the road with a bamboo staff you have cut beforehand. Also, a staff with a cover for a spear handle will do nicely. With this, wild animals will run away.

Also, if you walk along carrying a woven cord of bamboo or cypress bark infused with saltpeter and lit at the end, or a torch made of pine resin, you will not encounter wild animals.

Beyond that, if you walk along mountain paths with some cow dung smeared on the bottoms of your straw sandals, wild animals, snakes, vipers and poisonous insects will be afraid and not approach you.

If you place picture talismans of *Gogaku** or *Hakutaku*** in your breast pocket, you will invite no disasters during your travels, and demons and fierce beasts will not approach you.

Various strange occurances that are the tricks of badgers and foxes*** include your suddenly being lost on the road, it quickly beoming dark, a river appearing where there really is none, or a closed gate where there was no gate before. Should you encounter such things, first calm yourself, smoke a little tobacco or rest, and try to recall the road by which you came. If you still do not understand the situation, retrace your steps, approach some human habitation and make inquiries. Doing this, you will not be tricked by foxes and badgers.

Keeping your mind calm in all events is essential in everything, not just while on a journey.

---

* Gogaku: A Chinese faith concerning holy mountains. The *gogaku* (五岳), or Five Mountains are *Ch'in shan* (the eastern peak), *Ch'ung shan* (the southern peak), *Hua shan* (the western peak), *Heng shan* (the northern peak) and *Sung shan* (the central peak).

** *Hakutaku*: The name of a Chinese mythological divine beast. It is capable of human speech, and its appearance predicts the reign of a virtuous king.

*** Badgers and foxes: Both are considered to be tracksters and shapeshifters in Japan.

Being Careful in a Boat

When boarding a boat, first place all the articles in the center of the craft, and ascertain where the removable floorboards and oars are stored. If strong wind or rain or a sudden gust should occur and the boat seems about to overturn, you should go into the water holding on to these oars and floorboards. Thus, even the person who cannot swim will be easily aided so as not to sink.

Out at sea, large fish will sometimes follow a boat. At such times, do not be alarmed, but if you will hide behind the ship's timber and strike it or anything else making a noise, the fish will go away.

There are times when a waterspout occurs near to the boat and black clouds suddenly spread out over a rough sea, waves boil up, and whirlpools appear. At such times, though the boatmen will understand the situation, without becoming alarmed, have them

throw things like the planking and straw matting into the whirl-pool to make it disappear. If this is done, the waves of the whirlpool will become calm. It is important that at that moment the boat rides through its difficulties.

It is not good that a boat carry a large group of people. First of all, the boarding of the boat is difficult. Then, the men who row the boat will have a tough time doing their job. At any rate, once in the boat, you should leave everything to the boatmen and never disobey them. There is a set way to do everything in a boat, and though there are grudges and adversities [among the passengers], it is most important not to bother the boatmen.

An Excellent Way to Deal with

Being Seasick

When someone is sick on a boat and has thrown up a great deal, his throat will be dry. At that time, have him drink the stools from a child. If no child is there, have him drink an adult's urine. If he makes the mistake of drinking water, he may die immediately. Please be careful with this.

When you board a boat, drink a mouthful of water from the river and you will not get sick on the boat.

When you board a boat, if you will wrap a little bit of soil from the earth, and place it above your navel, you will not get seasick.

If you wrap some sulphur in paper and put in your breast pocket, you will not get sick in a boat.

If you take two or three small slices of wood with the tips doused in suphur, put them gently in your breast pocket, and secrete them aboard, you will not get sick on the boat.

Also, drinking a mouthful of strong vinegar is good, as is putting a pickled plum in your mouth. Drinking the juice squeezed from a raw *daikon* is good as well.

If you are terribly seasick and cannot control your vomiting, it is good to boil equal portions of jack-in-the-culprit (*Pinellia ternate Breit*), the skin of a ripe mandarin orange and tuckahoe (*poria cocos*), and to drink the concoction.

How Not to Get Sick in a Palanquin

The person who gets sick in a palanquin should open the palanquin door and ride in this way.

Set a leaf of *nanten* (*Nandina domestica*) upright inside the palanquin, look at it as you go along, and you will not get sick. For a person with a terrible headache or who is feeling unwell, you should have him drink hot water mixed with an extract of ginger. Do not let him drink cold water.

When a woman mounts a horse or rides in a palanquin, she should wrap a sash tightly around the pit of her stomach.*

---

* *Mizuochi* can be translated as either the "pit of the stomach, " or the "solar plexus."

Treatment for Falling off a Horse

If you fall off a horse, feel unwell and your saliva is tinged with blood, it is best to drink sake with powdered lotus root. You can also mix powdered lotus leaf with sake. Again, if your hips or feet suffered a heavy blow and are covered with black and blue marks, go quickly to a clinic and have blood drawn. If you do this, you will not need treatment later. Beyond that, it is good to have a massage.

A horse's sweat is extremely poisonous. Do not let it get in your food or eyes.

How to Avoid Poisonous Insects

I t is good to carry a [small] fragrant bag in your breast pocket. It is also good to carry powdered *kanshou* and *oou** in the same place. At any rate, you will do well to carry something highly aromatic like Sumatra camphor, deer musk or camphor from the laurel tree in your breast pocket.

---

* 乾姜 and 雄黄. Neither could be identified. The first may be dried ginger.

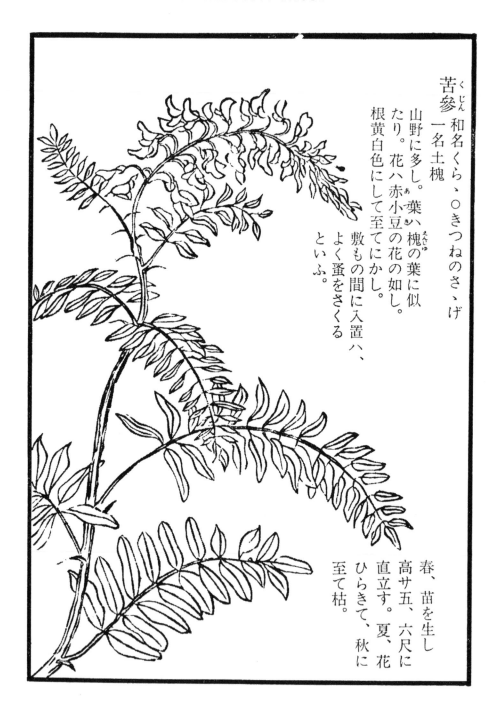

苦参（くじん）　和名くら、〇きつねのさゝげ
一名土槐

山野に多し。葉ハ槐（ゑんじゆ）の葉に似
たり。花ハ赤小豆の花の如し。
根黄白色にして至てにかし。

敷もの間に入置ハ、
よく蚤をさくる
といふ。

春、苗を生し
高サ五、六尺に
直立す。夏、花
ひらきて、秋に
至て枯。

50

How to Avoid Fleas in Inns on the Road

F leas will not approach if you place a fresh grass called *kujin* (苦参 *Sophora flavescens Ait.*) over your upper futon. This plant grows widely in the mountains and fields, so be mindful of this as you walk along, break off some and put it on your futon. I include an illustration of *kujin* in this book. Study it well.

If you take along one fruit of the trifoliate orange (*Citrus trifoliate*; also called a Bengal quince) and hold it as you sleep at night, fleas will not draw near.

It is also good to put some dried knotweed (*Polygonum caespitosum* var. laxiflorum) under your bed.*

Also, if you dip your undergarments in a large quantity of boiled knotweed seeds then hang them out to dry, fleas will avoid you when you put them on.

---

* The reader should be warned however, that it would seem that not all insects avoid this plant. A Japanese saying has it that *Tade kuu mushi mo sukisuki*—蓼食う虫も好きすき. "Every man to his taste," or "There is no accounting for taste."

51

Novel Ways and Secret Formulas
for Treating Fatigue on the Road

When you rest at a tea house, do not sit down dangling your feet with your footwear still on your feet. Take your footwear off for a little while, sit down on a bench or something similar, and rest with proper posture. This will cure your fatigue in a marvelous way.

When someone who is new at travelling becomes fatigued or gets blisters on his feet, it is almost always due to his being indifferent about the way he puts on his footwear. Obtain good footwear, beat them until they are soft, do not put them on in hurry, and make sure they are neither too tight nor too loose. Also, when your feet are dry and hot, they will hurt and develop blisters. Therefore, from time to time loosen the laces to your footwear, cool your hot feet, and rest in a proper posture.

When you are tired and your feet hurt, after you've reached your inn and taken a bath, rub an ample amount of salt on the soles of your feet and warm them by a fire. This is remarkably efficacious.

When you are extraordinarily fatigued, blow some *shochu** from just below your knees to the soles of your feet. Rubbing it in with your hand will have no effect.

When you walk a long distance and the arches of your feet become swollen and hurt, it's best to mash up earthworms with the mud still on them and rub them onto your arches.

When you have become fatigued, it is good to have moxabustion just below your knee, at mid calf, and on the side of your little toe. Please look at the following illustration.

When you develop blisters on the soles of your feet, knead some jack-in-the-culprit powder in with some grains of boiled rice, and rub the concoction onto [the afflicted area].

Kneading tobacco ashes with grains of boiled rice, and then heating the mixture also works well.

You can also obtain some *To no tsuchi*** at a pharmacy. Knead this together with just a few grains of boiled rice, and rub the mixture onto the affected area.

Again, you may take a needle threaded with a cotton thread, thoroughly wet the thread with some ink from an ink stone, and pierce the side of the blister. Water will then be released, but the ink will remain inside the blister, and this will stop the pain to a surprising degree.

You may also dissolve *udon* noodle powder into some water, and rub that on the blistered area.

When you are travelling during the summer, and the bottoms of your feet get hot and hurt, rub the leaves of knotweed, and the blue-green liquid onto the afflicted area.

---

* A Japanese hard liquor distilled from sweet potatoes, rice, or almost anything available.

** *To no tsuchi*: A white powder of carbolic acid mixture used in Chinese medicine.

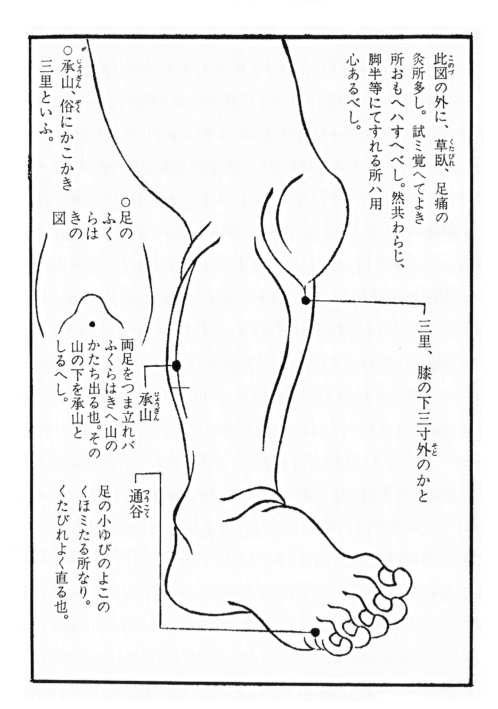

此図の外に、草臥、足痛の灸所多し。試ミ覚へてよき所おもへハすへべし。然共わらじ、脚半等にてすれる所八用心あるべし。

三里、膝の下三寸外のかと

○承山、俗にかこかき三里といふ。

○足のふくらはきのの図

両足をつま立れバふくらはきへ山のかたち出る也。その山の下を承山としるべし。

承山

通谷

足の小ゆびのよこのくほミたる所なり。くたびれよく直る也。

When you are on the road during the summer, placing the leaf of a peach tree under your bamboo hat will alleviate the sensation of heat in a marvelous way.

If you imbibe one or two grains of pepper every morning, you will not be affected by the summer heat. In the winter, you will not encounter blizzards.

When you drink water in the summertime, it is good to crush a grain of pepper between your teeth. Also, if you "chew" water when you drink it, you will not be affected by it.

When you are stung by a poisonous insect, rub either *enreitan** or *sokou'en*** on the sting, the pain will be alleviated immediately.

If you broil mud snails in soy sauce, dry them, carry the potion along with you as you travel towards your destination, and take a mouthful every two or three days, you will not be affected by [the change] of water.

---

* *Enreitan*: A stimulant used during Roan's time as a regular household medicine. Composed of cinnamon, an aromatic, aloes, cinnabar, honey and about ten other ingredients.

** *Sokou'en*: A concoction of a number of ingredients, rolled into a pill. Taken to eliminate phlegm and as an insecticide and an antiseptic.

How Not to be Affected by Steam

When a person is in the bathtub for a long time and is affected by the hot steam, he should spray cold water on his face. If he has a nosebleed that won't stop and extreme dizziness, he should pour [cool] water over his entire body.

Moreover, after he has sprayed his face with water, if he will untie his hair and comb it a number of times with a wide-spaced comb, he will feel remarkably better. He could also drink a little bit of vinegar.

Good Medicines to Take on a Trip

This chapter lists a number of tradition Chinese medicines (*kanpoyaku*), and their uses. It would be tedious and unprofitable to list all of their ingredients, and most of these medicines would be difficult to come by except—perhaps—at traditional kanpoyaku pharmacies, which, however, can be found throughout Japan. For those interested, they are the following:

- *Kuma no i* (熊の胆), *Kiougan* (奇応丸), *Hankoutan* (反魂丹).
  Used to counter convulsions, stomach aches, upset stomach, sunstroke, and general stomach complaints.

- *Goreisan* (五苓散), *Koshou* (胡椒).
  Used for changes in water, and for drinking any water when the throat is dry during summer travel.

- *San'outou* (三黄湯).
  Used for constipation.

- *Kirimogusa* (切もぐさ).
  To prevent dampness.

- *Bikyuu'en* (備急円).
  To prevent vomiting and diarrhea in the case of extreme upset stomach.

- *Aburagusuri* (油薬), *Hakuryuukou* (白龍膏), *Baikakou* (梅花香), *Keikakou* (桂花香).
  For cuts, swelling and bites from poisonous insects.

Two others, not known during Roan's time, are available even in modern drug stores in Japan. The first, *Seirogan*, was developed during the Sino-Japanese war; the latter, *Hyakusogan*, is a speciality around Mt. Ontake and is sold all along the Kiso Road.

- *Seirogan* (正露丸).
  This commonly used *kanpoyaku* is taken as treatment for stomach disorders such as stomach aches, diarrhea, food poisoning, and intake of contaminated water. Its main ingredients are: wood creosote (also called beechwood creosote), powdered gambir leaves, Amur corktree bark, and Chinese licorice root.

- *Hyakusougan* (百草丸).
  This is taken primarily for stomach and intestinal problems such as lack of appetite, after effects of excessive eating and drinking, heavy stomach, nausea, bloating, indigestion, heartburn and vomiting.

Personal Effects for Travelling

- Ink and brush case, a folding fan, needle and thread, a pocket mirror, a daily notebook (one volume), a comb and hair oil.
  A razor for cutting hair can be borrowed and used at one's inn. Your hair will need to be tied up and arranged, but when it is not arranged well, it can be corrected upon request along the way at barriers or in castle towns.

- A paper lantern, candles, flint and steel, and pocket tinder. This last should be carried even by those who do not smoke. The lamps in inns are easily blown out, so you should have something for the unexpected.

- Hempen rope. This can be used for tying up luggage at the post towns. It is extraordinarily convenient.

- Wooden impression of your seal.
  Leaving your own seal at home, this can used to compare the seal with letters sent from places on your trip; it can also be used as a seal when changing gold and silver.

Writing a Journal on the Road

A s for the famous places and ancient sites you visit on the road, or wonderful scenery and things you have seen and heard about—write down the plain facts of the dates, location, and what you actually saw. If Chinese poetry, tanka, linked poetry or haiku should come to your mind, you should write them down in your journal any way you can, even if you cannot think of some parts or the proper order of the poems.

When sketching the scenery of mountains and rivers, you should draw them just as they are. You can make a clean copy at a later date after you've returned home. Trying to make your poetry perfect or your paintings beautiful while on the road will hinder your trip, and will not have good results anyway. Be careful about this.

Looking at Weather Patterns/
Old Poems and Sayings

R ain that falls around twelve at night, eight in the morning or around five in the evening will continue for some time.

When rain falls around ten in the morning or six in the evening, there will be good weather soon.

When rain falls around nine at night, four in the morning or just at noon, it will only sprinkle and soon will cease.

Finally, rain falling around two in the afternoon, six in the evening (*sic*), or ten at night will come down hard and last for half a day.

There should be rain with wind from the east, but when such a wind blows during the rainy season or midsummer, it is a sign that a continuing rain will soon let up.

- When a sudden squall comes from the east, it is proof that the evening will be clear.
- During the spring and summer, a wind blowing from the northwest is an indication of coming rain.
- When the wind blows from the west during the autumn, rain is certain.
- When the wind blows from the south during the winter, there will be three days of frost.
- A west or northwest wind means clear skies. An east or south wind brings the rain.
- When the sky is red or blue as the sun sets, it will get windy. If the clouds are red in the evening, it will clear up. If the clouds are moving in a disorderly fashion, there will be strong winds. If wind and clouds are gone without a trace, the rain will stop. If the colors of the clouds are red and white, there will be a typhoon.
- When there is mist at night, the following day will have strong winds.
- When a shooting star moves to the east, there will be wind. If stars are visible within the halo of the moon, it will rain. When there is a multiple halo, there will be strong winds. When the moon is sinking and releases a strong light, it will rain; when its color is white, there will be wind. When a rainbow appears in the west in the morning, there will be three days of rain. If there is a rainbow in the eastern sky during the evening, there will be clear weather. When there is lightning running in all four directions, there will be a driving rain.
- When it looks like rain, the house's foundation stones will be bathed in moisture.

- When the mountains can be seen clearly, there will be an easterly wind. When the mountains are hidden and cannot be seen, the wind will be from the north.
- When crows are bathing themselves, it is a sure indication of rain.*
- When doves are cooing and there are answering calls, the weather will be clear. If there are no answering coos, it is a sign of rain.
- If kites cry in the morning, it will rain. If they cry in the evening, it will be clear.
- If smoke from the cooking stove is gloomy and sinks in a downward direction, you may well think it might rain. If the smoke rises straight up, there will be clear weather.

The ways of predicting the weather according to the coming and going of the clouds will be different in the various parts of the country. In Osaka, when overhanging clouds are moving towards the northeast, they call them *irigumo,* or clouds going in. These are clouds carrying rain.

Again, when the clouds are moving towards the southwest, they call them *degumo,* or clouds coming out. These also indicate rain, but when they are accompanied by strong winds, there will be good weather . . .

The climate and weather changes from area to area, so you cannot make generalities. But by and large, in the Kanto [the area around Tokyo], if a west wind is blowing, the weather will be clear; if an east wind is blowing, it will rain. In the Kansai [the area around Kyoto and Osaka], if a west wind is blowing, it will rain; if an east wind is blowing, it will be clear. Thus, be careful to inquire about local conditions.

---

* When crows caw, the weather will change. (Saying from Nagano Prefecture.) When crows make their nests on low branches, it will be a year of strong winds. (Common saying)

Old poems and sayings

When Mt. Chikuba is clear,
    Mt. Asama clouds over,
And the shrike cries,
        Though it rains   Let your journey begin.

Know that a west wind in
    In the Fifth Month, a southern wind in the spring
        A north wind in the fall,
    And a constant wind
        from the east all mean rain.

A north wind in the spring
    A southerly wind in the winter,
    Or a constant wind from the east
    With these for sure
        A light rain will fall.

The mist slipping
        down the mountain
Will bring sunshine;
        Mist climbing up
        Will bring rain.

The latter two poems are good for forecasting the weather. It is certain than when a mist is descending, the weather will be clear, and when the mist is rising, there will be rain. This writer has tested them, and they are never wrong. Plus, they are easy to remember.

ものゝふの
やはせの
わたし
ちかく
とも
いそかは
まはれ
瀬田の
長橋

The first two poems must have been based on weather in the Kanto district. But in all ways of looking at the weather, be it predicting rain and wind according to the movement of the clouds on Mt. Fuji or Chikuba in the Kanto, know the situation by using your own eyes in province to province and place to place.

Finally, when you depart on a journey, you should inquire about conditions wherever you are. The good and bad weather on the road can make or break your trip. Be especially thoughtful about conditions when wading across a river or boarding a boat.

Instructional Poems on Travel

When taking an inn
    At first, get your bearings,
Then find the lavatory,
    How to secure your door,
    And finally, the source of fire.

Do not think,
    "I'll go as I please!"
When taking a journey.
    Rather, think, "I may have some problems;"
    The you'll be free as a bird.

On a long journey
    Don't take too much gear;
Settle on just a few things
    Take a lot and you'll suffer
    In equal measure.

He who would take
    Matters lightly on the road,
Will only think of river crossings
    And other disasters
    When they are right before his eyes.

Early setting out,
    Early taking an inn,
The man on the road
    Will encounter
    No disasters.

When on the road,
    Do not eat much at one time,
But rest, then rest again,
    And take a bite to eat
    Any time you like.

The traveler who declares
    the cuisine where he stops
To be good or bad,
    Will never understand
    The places he's been.

The man who tastes
    the customs and conditions
Of the places he travels through
    Will have wonderful meals,
    Though it be rough fare.

Even if you hold your liquor well,
    Do not drink heavily
On a journey.
    But a little from time to time
    Is good medicine.

Though you be in a hurry
    To reach your destination,
Never cross unfamiliar rivers
    Or shortcuts
    You don't know.

If it occurs to you offhand,
    "I should take a boat,"
Think first:
    Will this speed my journey,
    Or slow it down?

On a rainy day, take lodging
    While the sky is still bright.
Waiting 'til dark,
    Good inns
    Will already be filled.

On the road,
    Though you have
Retainers and coolies,
    Do what needs to be done
    Yourself.

Know this:
	When on the road,
He who travels in splendid attire
		Will meet with unpleasantness
		Without fail.

If a fire breaks out
	Close by your lodging,
First look for an exit
		Then collect
		Your gear.

While on a journey
	Speak with quiet and calm.
Avoid arguments,
		Quibbling,
		And talking out loud.

Do not show off your talents
	While on the road.
By hiding them
		Your light will shine
		All the more.

When crossing a river
	Or boarding a boat,
Be mindful not to drop
		Your valuables
		Or purse.

Show no disrespect
    To horse packers, coolies and such.
Everyone travels
    The same weary world,
    The same human life.

During a journey,
    Restrain yourself
Though your anger be hot.
    Say what needs to be said
    At a later time.

When riding a horse
    Loaded with gear,
Mount only after
    Even the small packages
    Have been accounted for.

When leaving
    Your night's lodging,
Be careful with each other's baggage
    So that nothing
    Will be left behind.

    If people will frequently recite these instructional poems on travel
by heart, they will become useful knowledge when on the road at a
later date.

Poems for Departure

I'll put a small dedicated sprig
>To the god of travel*
In the garden,
>And pray until your safe
>Return.

You cannot determine [by divination]
>A lucky day to start your trip.
As for good and evil,
>Make that lucky day
>The day you decide to go.

---

* Asuba no kami (阿須波の神): also known as the god of a house and the land on which it stands.

Japan's Hot Springs

ong before there were doctors of medicine in our country, O-namuchi no mikoto and Sukunahito no mikoto travelled around the various provinces looking for hot springs that would cure the sick and soothe the grief of people who had lost children. Since that time, these hot springs have been visited for the amelioration of illnesses. And from that time on to this very day, hot springs treatment has been popular among people of both high and low classes.

- With their marvelous natural power, hot springs can moisten the skin, loosen the joints, circulate the blood, and strengthen the function of the internal organs. Thus, the people who take this treatment believe in the efficacy of hot springs, and use them with devotion.

白澤圖

此白澤の図を懐中すれバ、善事をすゝめて悪事をしれぞけ、山海の災難、病患をまぬかれ、開運昇進の祥瑞あること古今云伝ふる所也。因而旅中ハ最尊信あるべし。

- Concerning the efficacy of hot springs, when at an unfamiliar location, be sure to ask local people [about the baths] and then take your treatment. There are hot springs both fitting and unfitting, according to one's ailment, and this fact should not be treated lightly.

- When going to a hot spring, you should determine whether it is efficacious or not for your own particular ailment. If your appetite increases and your food tastes good after you have gotten into the water once or twice, then you can be assured that this hot spring will be good for you. If, however, your stomach becomes tight and your appetite does not increase with the same number of immersions, it will probably not be fitting in your case. At any rate, if you have discussed your ailment in detail before you visit a hot spring location, you should feel secure in entering the baths. Well then, after two or three days of bathing, you will naturally know yourself if the hot spring is right for you or not.

- The method of bathing in a hot spring is the following: For the first day or two, enter the bath three or four times a day. If it feels right, then go in anywhere from five to seven times. The old and weak should adjust themselves accordingly. In the case of chronic ailments, just going to the bath once will not work as a treatment; you should take the treatment many times, perhaps even for a month or two.

- While you are at a hot spring, whether you are sick or healthy, you should be circumspect about over-eating, drinking too much, sexual conduct and consuming cold foods. Moreover, on getting out of the bath, all the pores of your body are open, so it is easy to become cold. Thus, when you are deep in the mountains, you should not expose your body to chilly breezes, cool your feet in water, or sleep in places where there is a draft. You can become very chilled when getting out of a bath, so be careful.

- The hot springs are the best that are indeed hot and transparent enough to see to the bottom like a mirror. Those that are just luke warm, dirty or with a strange color cannot be said to be of the highest class. Nevertheless, there are hot springs that are not clear or have a strange color that will do no harm; and if they feel good or are efficacious with your own ailment, you cannot generalize too much.

- Also, even though there may be several hot spring establishments set up around the spring's single source, the hot water of each place will have a different efficacy. Therefore, if you visit a location with several hot spring establishments, be sure to ask a number of questions at each one. Every famous hot spring will either be appropriate or not appropriate according to the ailment. It is always best to be careful and ask.

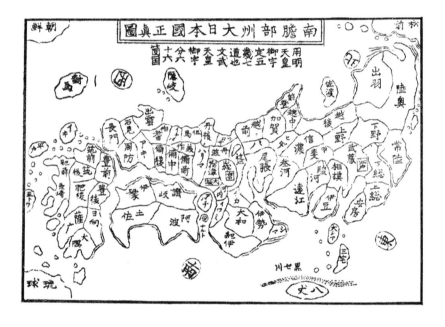

List of Illustrations

> Walking on and on
> they become flowers on
> on branches:
> as we see clearly
> the snows on the peak.

pp. 19, 20:   Illustrations of poisonous snakes and insects. The text states,
There are many poisonous plants and insects you may
encounter in the fields and plains during the summer, and
you should note these by all means. Among these, the viper
called *mamushi* (*Agkistrodon blomhoffi*) and the beetle called
the *hanmyo* (*Cicindela japonica*) are extremely poisonous,
and everyone should be aware of these two. Other than
them, there are insects that are generally not poisonous, but
become so according to the season, and their poison is no
weaker than that of scorpions and snakes. Thus, you must
be careful about gnats, mosquitoes, wasps, bees, ants, caterpillars, spiders and leeches. In warm areas, the humidity
and heat can be especially severe, and there are numerous
poisonous plants and strange insects. In this way, if the
traveler becomes tired and rests in the fields or mountains,
he should be very careful. Good medicines for countering
the stings of poisonous insects are written down elsewhere.

The illustrated insects, snakes, etc. below the text are
from, from right to left:

The yellow *Kara no hanmyo*, or Chinese Tiger Beetle,

The bright blue *Wa no hanmyo*, or Japanese Tiger Beetle,

A lizard called the *Tokage* in Japanese, but various named
the *Ishi warawa* or *Yama warawa*,

A black snake called the *Usha*, or *Karasu hebi* (*Natrix pryeri*),

The above-noted mamushi, also called the *Fukuhami* or
Hanbija. The color of this snake is black/green, and there
are many varieties. Their poison is extremely strong.

p. 25:   A poem by Nijo Tameshige.

Cross over
the cloud-covered hill
between the patches of rain;
though close
to Mt. Mikasa.

p. 26:   A poem by Minamoto Yorimasa.

Though green leaves

could still be seen

when leaving the capital,

autumn leaves were falling

at the Shirakawa barrier.

p. 32:   A poem by Minamoto Morotoki

With snow falling, every mountain

grows higher;

how will I know

Mt. Shirane,

the one I must cross.

p. 35:   An illustration of winter transport

p. 43:   An illustration of the dangers of travel by ship

p. 50:   An illustration of *kujin*. The text reads:

Kujin. In Japan it is also called *kurara*, or more commonly, *kitsune no sasage*, or *enju*. It grows luxuriantly in the mountains and fields, and the leaves are similar to those of the enju, or Japanese pagoda tree.

Its flowers are like the flowers of red beans, the root is yellowish white, and is very bitter. It is said that if you put it between your upper and lower futon, it will be a bane to fleas.

In the spring, the buds grow straight up five or six feet. The flowers open during the summer, and the plant withers in the fall.

p. 54:   Points for the application of moxa. The test reads:

Besides those in the illustration, there are many points for the application of moxa that are efficacious for countering fatigue and sore feet. It is good to test them out to find what you think best. But do not apply moxa in places where it would rub against footwear or gaiters.

The points are, first at the right and then left, top to bottom:

Sanri: About three inches below the outside corner of the knee.

Sanri: Commonly called the "Three *ri* of the palanquin bearer."

An illustration of the calf.

Shozan: When standing on tiptoe with both feet, the calf will take the shape of a mountain. The point, shozan, is just below that mountain.

Tsukoku: This is the depressed area just to the side of the little toe.

Apply moxa here to treat fatigue.

p. 66: Anonymous poem

Warriors!

Though close to the crossing

at Yahase,

if in a hurry, go around,

take the long bridge at Seta.

p. 75: The Shirazawa Talisman. The text reads:

If you put this illustration of Shirazawa in your breast pocket, you will promote good things and avoid bad ones. You will evade disasters in the mountains and seas, sidestep illnesses, and open up good luck. This omen has been circulated in times present and times past. Thus, it should be regarded with extreme respect and faith while travelling.

p. 78: An old map of Japan and its provinces

Appendix

Further Notes on Travel

Tokaido meishoki (1658)

- For travel, a companion; out in the world, fellow feeling.

- The first thing in travel is medicine; it is essential to guard against illness.

- Be circumspect about fruit, cold water and carelessly chosen food.

- During summer travel, cholera (sunstroke?) often occurs from spoiled food.

- If you travel together with suspicious people and stay in the same inn, they may secretly change baggage with you, or take your baggage while you sleep.

- If you leave your inn at night, be careful of robbers and street murderers.

- At your inn, be mindful of the conditions of the place and the strategic back alleyways.

- You should not lean your baggage against the walls in the waiting room. If there are places where the tatami is sunken or seems to be weak, lift it up and inspect it.

- Where you sleep at night, place the hilt of your sword at your side.

- Don't play around with prostitutes and let them steal your money. Even if they call on you, don't loosen your guard.

- There is nothing that excels patience when you are on the road. Boatmen, pack horsemen, and men leading oxcarts are liable to prattle on like the rattling of leaves and do as they please. Not to be overcome by this is extremely important.

- Do not place fans, umbrellas or purses in high places. They are easily forgotten.

- You should not hand over your money for the inn at night. Pay in the morning.

- When there are shrines or Buddhist temples at the side of the road, fold your hands together reverently in prayer and pass by.

Soho kairiku kotei saikenki (1836)

- If you board a ferry for a sea crossing or get into a boat for some other reason, it is essential that you understand that rough winds may suddenly occur. Thus, you should always tie your sash in front. If there is some mishap and you should fall in the water, you will be able to quickly untie your sash and get out of your clothes [so they won't drag you down].

- You should understand that you can be pushed along by the current of a river, and [will not be able to swim] as you wish.

- On the road, do not pass by another person on your left. Should you encounter an upper class person, be all the more prepared to let him pass by on the right.

- During travel, it's best to get up early in the morning and finish your breakfast. And, if you depart a little earlier than usual, you will not be anxious or in a hurry on the road, but can walk at your leisure. In the same way, you should stop earlier in the afternoon and take your lodging.

- You should use a staff when you walk over a mountain pass or up a steep slope. If you walk along swaying back and forth, your feet will never hurt.

- On your travels back and forth, even if there is a shortcut, do not be too quick to take it. And you should be especially careful at night. Do not walk along the narrow pathways between rice fields or cross plank bridges in dim light.

- On the road, you may fall in with people who look like merchants or travelers who will chat you up and recommend that you purchase medicines, valuables or other things that they have come by. You should use great caution in such cases. Quicken your pace, and leave such people behind.

- When you suddenly experience stomach pains or your feet hurt, if an unknown person should offer you medicine, do not be too quick to take it. You should be very careful about this, and have your own medicine at hand for just such occasions.

- How not to fall off of a horse: When you are about to mount a horse, before taking hold of the reins, write the Chinese character for south (南) on the palm of your hand so no one can see it. Then mount the horse and you will not fall off.

- How to deal with blisters on your feet: There are various kinds of medicines for blisters, but if the blisters do not heal quickly, you will be very inconvenienced. Here is an excellent treatment, and you should lay it in store ahead of time. Char the seeds of a Nishikouri persimmon*, spread it out and knead it. The pain will cease quickly; a miraculous cure. It will not come off, even if you put [your foot] in water.

---

* Nishikouri kaki (西郡柿): I have not been able to identify this kind of persimmon.

Enoshima moude, hama no sazanami (1839)

- When you first depart from your lodging, walk in a leisurely fashion, and take very good care of your feet. Be careful not to stumble over small stones or roots, and be of a mind not to become tired out.

- When you have gone three or four *ri*[*] on the road, you may not feel comfortable with the condition of your footwear. At such a time, immediately loosen and then re-tie the thongs, making sure that they are tight. Poor footwear should be quickly removed and exchanged [for something of better quality]. For the traveler, footwear is his armor and helmet. Do not be niggling about the price, for you must have good footwear. If you walk about with poor footwear, the thongs will soon cut into your feet, and you'll start getting tired. You should know that there is no worse affliction than this.

- Even if you carry but a small amount of money, you should wrap it up in your waistband. This is a secret for not carrying it in your pocket. If by any chance you should drop other important documents and such, you should retrace your steps right away. A traveler should be careful about such things.

- When travelling alone, or even with company, you should make your baggage as light as possible. Even with only a two or three day journey, you should prepare yourself with raingear. With continuing fair weather, anyone would think this to be bothersome; but when it suddenly starts to rain on the road, [those without raingear] will be in bad shape. Moreover, when travelling alone, put a sheet of oilpaper in your bundle. In an emergency it could be as valuable as a precious jewel.

---

[*]   *Ri*: 2.44 miles.

- On the road, there are always people who [aggressively] offer the services of horses or palanquins at the entrances and exits of station towns. Even if you do not need such services, you should never decline them rudely or walk around with an air of ridicule for those who would. Have no doubts that such is the cause of fights. You should be very cautious about this.

- There will be *tome'onna** who try to pull you into their inns, and who will not listen even if you refuse and tell them that you already have lodging for the night. In a moment, four or five of them may appear, forcefully take you by the hand or sleeve and pull you towards their establishment. Even if such a thing should happen, to strike these women or yell and act violently with them is the worst way of dealing with the situation. When they've wrapped themselves around you and seized you and your belongings, go along meekly to their establishment; and if you already have arranged for lodging, inform them of its name, declare that as you must settle in early and indicate that you must repair to this place now. If you thus calmly put them off, they will have no other recourse [than to let you go].

- When you arrive at your inn and go into the bath, you're fine as long as you are with companions or friends. But if you are alone, you should wrap up your purse, waistband, wallet and other small packages in a *furoshiki*** and take them to the bath with you. Cover that with your clothes, put it in a place you can see, and enter the bath. You should have this understanding for the inns you enter day by day.

---

* Women who try to pull travelers into the inns where they are employed for the night.

** *Furoshiki*: a large cloth wrapper or kerchief.

- When you have arrived at your inn, taken your bath, eaten your meal and prepared for the next day, ask for a portable candle-holder and a candle. This is for finding your way to the toilet late at night, for some inns will not have candles in the bathroom.* Even if you arrive at your inn during the evening and feel no need, you should clearly locate the urinal and the toilet.

- You should be extremely circumspect about calling in one of the ladies or prostitutes of the inn and carrying on wantonly. This is not just a matter of the affliction of syphilis or fungus. You should make circumspection your greatest concern during your journey, for when your mind becomes lax, it is the beginning of the breakdown of things. Other things you should be particularly careful about on the road are visits to shrines, negotiations and going to hot springs. You should be careful about your body during all of these. Should you not take care of your health all along the way?

- Although merchants are different, you should be hesitant about sharing a room with a warrior or some elegant person. Even at an increased cost, you will be more at ease with your own room. If you must be with others during the summer, sleep under your own mosquito net and you will feel more comfortable.

- On the road, you should eat about half of what you would in ordinary times; and you should go forward a bit, then eat. Eating a lot at one time is not good at all. Look at people like couriers or runners, eating light single dishes at a time. And the same with sake: you should drink only a third of what you might drink on an ordinary day. Especially with treats like mochi cakes, dumplings, steamed rice with red beans, and sweet potatoes, you should not eat to satiety.

---

* Here, bathroom means the room with the toilet.

- When you arrive at your lodging, look carefully at the land-scape, the structure of the building, the location of the toilet, and the entrances and exits. Also, check the opening and closing of the sliding doors—whether they move easily or not. This is so that in case of a nearby fire, a thief or a fight, you will not be at a loss.

- When a bridge is washed away by a flood, or what was once a small stream is suddenly wider from bank to bank, by all means, hire a *kawagoshi*.* You should rely on such people regardless of the fare. Never take a small stream lightly. In short, to try to wade across a stream you are not familiar with is the very heart of foolishness.

---

* *Kawagoshi*: A man hired to carry people over a river on his back.

Naniwa kotei yadocho (1852)

- You should not drink a lot of sake on the road. And of course, you should never drink with people you have fallen in with on the road. People have different ways about them, and this can invite much trouble. You should be careful about this.

- Though a traveler you have fallen in with on the road offers you food, you should not lightly partake of it. By and large, you should have no business with travelers with whom you are not familiar. If such a person gets into trouble, you may become involved as well, and his trouble will become yours.

- Even if the fare for an inn is inexpensive, do not take lodging there if there is something questionable about the place. Moreover, you should never fall in with a single woman you meet travelling on the road.

- Generally speaking, you should not go and look at a place where people are fighting or having a duel. And of course, you should never get involved yourself.

- You should be very circumspect about getting into arguments or heated discussions with packhorse leaders or coolies and the like while on the road.

- When the post town official comes to ask your name, you should not joke around or be deceptive. And you should state clearly the province from which you have come. This is the care you should take on the chance that you may fall ill or something on the road. Identity may be mistaken from the [wrong] name, and this can cause great trouble and confusion. And again, never put idle scribbling on the post town register.

- There are many other things you should understand [about travelling], but it is essential that you be circumspect, think carefully about the consequences of all that you do, and know that even trivial actions can end in uncertainty.

Bibliography

Works in Japanese

Yasumi Roan. *Ryoko yojinshu*. Tokyo: Yasaka shobo, 1972.
Yasumi Roan. *Ryoko yojinshu*.Tokyo: Yasaka shobo, 2009.

Works in English

Ikku Jippensha. *Hizakurige of Shank's Mare* (Translated by Thomas Satchell). Tokyo and Rutland, Vermont: Charles E. Tuttle Company, 1960.
Keene, Donald. *Travelers of a Hundred Ages*. New York: Columbia University Press, 1999
Kerouac, Jack. *The Dharma Bums*. New York: Viking Penguin, 2008
Lyons, Mathew. *Impossible Journeys*. London: Cadogan Guides, 2005.
Vaporis, Constantine Nomikos. *Breaking Barriers*. Cambridge, Massachusetts: Harvard University Press, 1994.

About the Translator

WILLIAM SCOTT WILSON, the translator, was born in 1944 and grew up in Fort Lauderdale, Florida. As an undergraduate student at Dartmouth College in 1966, he was invited by a friend to join a three-month kayak trip up the coast of Japan from Shimonoseki to Tokyo. This eye-opening journey, beautifully documented in *National Geographic*, spurred Wilson's fascination with the culture and history of Japan.

After receiving a B.A. degree in political science from Dartmouth, Wilson earned a second B.A. in Japanese language and literature from the Monterey Institute of Foreign Studies in Monterey, California, then undertook extensive research on Edo-period (1603-1868) philosophy at the Aichi Prefectural University, in Nagoya, Japan.

Wilson completed his first translation, *Hagakure*, while living in an old farmhouse deep in the Japanese countryside. *Hagakure* saw publication in 1979, the same year Wilson completed an M.A. in Japanese language and literature at the University of Washington. Wilson's other translations include *The Book of Five Rings*, *The Life-Giving Sword*, *The Unfettered Mind*, the Eiji Yoshikawa novel *Taiko*, and *Ideals of the Samurai*, which has been used as a college textbook on Japanese history and thought. Two decades after its initial publication, *Hagakure* was prominently featured in the Jim Jarmusch film *Ghost Dog*.

Wilson currently lives in Miami, Florida.